WORLD'S SCARIEST PLACES

TERRIFYING TALES OF EARTH'S MOST CHILLING PLACES

Written by Kelly Hargrave
Designed by Kat Peruyera

Copyright © 2018 Scholastic Inc.

Scholastic, Tangerine Press, and associated logos are trademarks and/or registered trademarks of Scholastic Inc.

Published by Tangerine Press, an imprint of
Scholastic Inc., 557 Broadway,
New York, NY 10012

10 9 8 7 6 5 4 3 2 1

ISBN: 978-1-338-25663-5

Printed in Jiaxing, China

an imprint of
SCHOLASTIC
www.scholastic.com

Cover designer: Ali Castro
Photo editor: Cynthia Carris

TABLE OF CONTENTS

Would you like to go on a real ghost hunt some day? Follow the table of contents to tour the world's scariest places. That's a lot of scary places! It makes you wonder if the room you're sitting in right now is haunted too.

North America

Europe

South America

SCARIEST PLACES IN THE WORLD

Explore haunted castles, spooky cemeteries, abandoned mental asylums, supernatural shipwrecks and more. Each bone-chilling site within these pages is REAL.

Each scary place has its own terrifying tale to go with it. Many people claim to have seen frightfully freaky ghosts and crazy creepy creatures. Some say they have heard spine-tingling screams and mysterious, luring music at midnight while the air around them turns shiveringly ice cold.

BEWARE!

Feel like you're being watched?

Use your special ghost-vision light throughout the book to discover what haunted objects and creatures might be lurking in the shadows.

The Castle of Good Hope,
Cape Town, South Africa

THE BELL
THAT RINGS ON ITS OWN

This castle is no stranger to spooky sights and haunted happenings. Take a walk on the grounds and you may hear the bell tower weirdly ringing on its own, even though the area the bell sits in was barricaded years ago. Legend says a soldier was hung from the bell rope, and now his tortured soul is responsible for the eerie, unexplainable chiming.

AFRICA

**CAPE TOWN,
SOUTH AFRICA**

The ghost of an angry governor roams the halls of the castle. It is said a soldier the governor executed put a curse on the governor's soul so that he would be doomed to never leave the castle.

A black dog will run straight for you but disappear as it gets close.

Voices and shuffling of feet can be heard in a space called the Dark Hole, which was once used as a torture chamber.

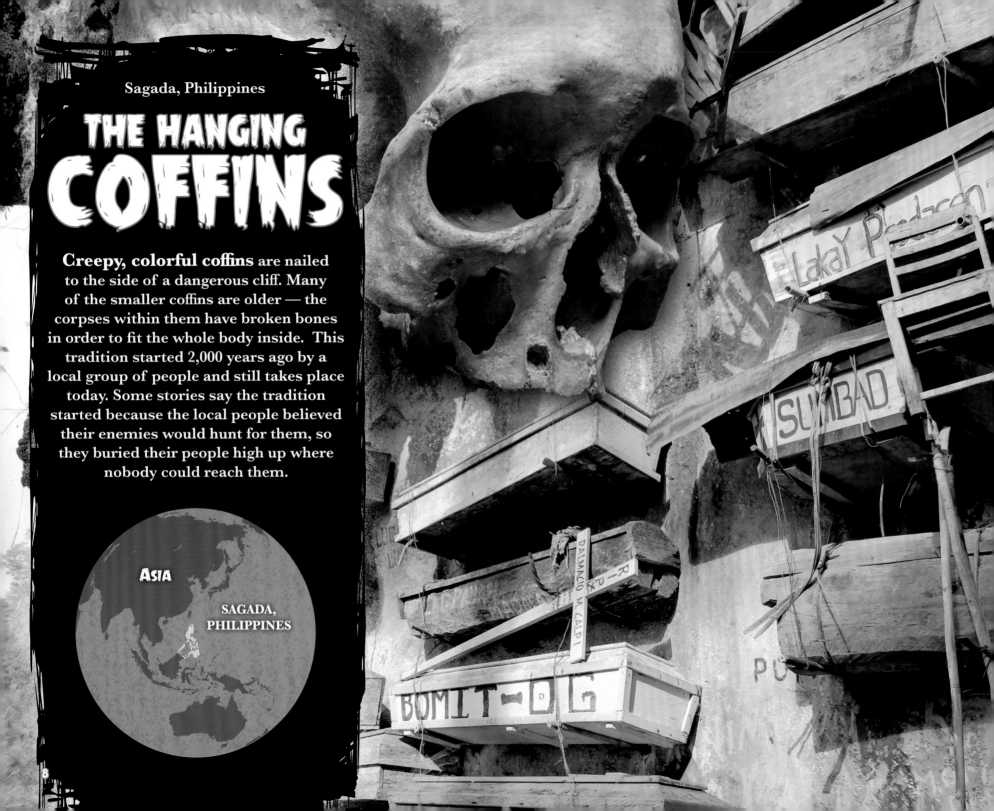

Sagada, Philippines

THE HANGING COFFINS

Creepy, colorful coffins are nailed to the side of a dangerous cliff. Many of the smaller coffins are older — the corpses within them have broken bones in order to fit the whole body inside. This tradition started 2,000 years ago by a local group of people and still takes place today. Some stories say the tradition started because the local people believed their enemies would hunt for them, so they buried their people high up where nobody could reach them.

ASIA

SAGADA,
PHILIPPINES

Another story says that burying them higher up brings them closer to the spirits of their ancestors.

And yet another story says that they feared dogs would eat them.

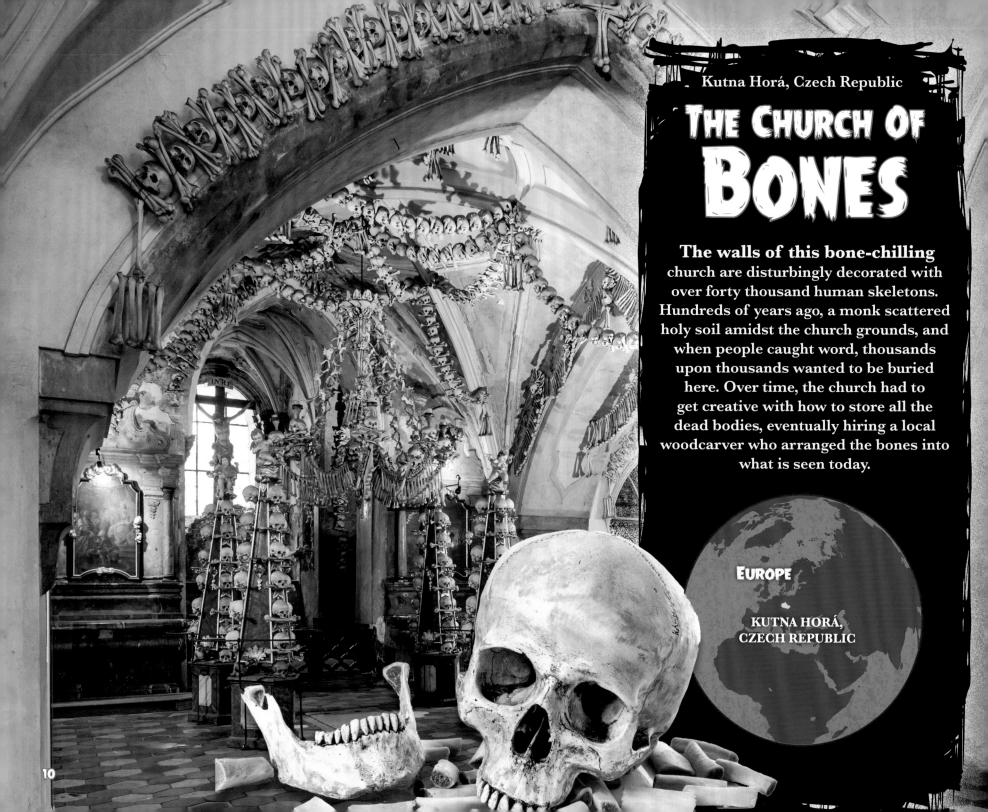

THE CHURCH OF BONES

The walls of this bone-chilling church are disturbingly decorated with over forty thousand human skeletons. Hundreds of years ago, a monk scattered holy soil amidst the church grounds, and when people caught word, thousands upon thousands wanted to be buried here. Over time, the church had to get creative with how to store all the dead bodies, eventually hiring a local woodcarver who arranged the bones into what is seen today.

EUROPE

KUTNA HORÁ, CZECH REPUBLIC

There is a chandelier that consists of at least one of every human bone in the body.

There are four candelabras made of bone and many candleholders made of skulls.

Khairatabad Science College, Hyderabad, India

The Walking SKELETONS

Believed to be one of the most haunted places in India, this dark and decrepit building used to be a science college. The biology lab was full of dead bodies for students to study. The story goes that when the building was abandoned, the dead bodies in the labs were not properly disposed and now their spooky skeletons can be seen walking the grounds.

ASIA

HYDERABAD, INDIA

Sparks and disturbing noises have also been heard.

A guard was stationed to watch over the building but he mysteriously died, adding to the building's already horrific happenings.

CRAZY CREEPY

Abandoned Amusement Parks

Once a place of fun and joy, these now-abandoned amusement parks will only give you spine-tingling chills.

Lake Shawnee Amusement Park, Princeton, West Virginia, USA

This park has long been closed after a few children died accidently, but its decaying structure still stands. People claim to have heard swings creaking when there is no wind and the looming laughter of children. The most notorious story is that of a little girl in a pink dress who died at the park and still haunts it. It is said when she stares at you, it is impossible to move.

NORTH AMERICA

PRINCETON, WEST VIRGINIA, USA

14

EUROPE

LANCASHIRE, ENGLAND

Camelot Theme Park, Lancashire, England

Walking through this abandoned amusement park, one may feel as if they have stumbled upon a mysterious mannequin graveyard. Each mannequin is more battered and bruised than the next, and they show very little sign of the characters they once played: noble knights, fair maidens, kings, queens, and wizards, all based on the renowned stories of King Arthur and his kingdom of Camelot.

CRAZY CREEPY

Abandoned Amusement Parks

NORTH AMERICA

NEW ORLEANS, LOUISIANA, USA

Six Flags, New Orleans, Louisiana, USA

This now-creepy wonderland of a park was only in business for 5 years before Hurricane Katrina nearly destroyed it and the bustling city around it. It never reopened due to too much wreckage, but it's proven to be the perfect spooky spot for directors to film scary movies.

Pripyat Amusement Park, Pripyat, Ukraine

A deathly nuclear explosion at a power plant in Pripyat caused the entire town to be evacuated due to high levels of radiation, leaving behind this rotting amusement park. Legend says days before the explosion, workers at the power plant saw a huge headless black, bird-like creature. It had the body of man and a 20-foot (6.10-m) wingspan. It disappeared after the explosion, causing many to believe the sight of the creature was a bad omen for what was to come.

EUROPE

PRIPYAT, UKRAINE

Vampire Water Mill, Zorazje, Serbia

Beware of the Butterfly Vampire

According to legend, this mysterious mill is said to belong to a vengeful vampire out for blood. When the vampire died, he took the sneaky shape of a butterfly and continued to haunt the mill. In 2012, the mill collapsed and the town went into a panic, believing the vampire was on the loose and looking for a new home. So be on the look out! If you see a butterfly, it could be a vampire looking for its next victim.

EUROPE

ZORAZJE, SERBIA

The sale of crosses and garlic went way up in the town when the mill collapsed.

ПРВИ СРПСКИ ВАМПИР САВА САВАНОВИЋ

3 KM

Because pumpkins and watermelons look like human heads, Serbian vampire lore says if a drop of blood is spotted on them, they will turn into vampires.

Larundel Mental Asylum,
Bundoora, Australia

THE MIDNIGHT MUSIC BOX

This graffiti-covered, abandoned asylum is riddled with suspicious supernatural activity. Brave a walk down its halls and you may get flashes of the sick and twisted patients that lived here. One story that haunts paranormal explorers is that of a girl who died on the third floor. She loved her music box very much, and to this day, people have claimed to hear spine-tingling music playing just before midnight.

AUSTRALIA

BUNDOORA, AUSTRALIA

Beware of mysterious banging on the walls.

Take a few more steps and you might just hear a spooky spirit crying.

THE FLOATING VAMPIRE OF HIGHGATE CEMETERY

The Highgate Vampire roams this cemetery along with other ghouls and ghosts. He is said to be a tall, thin, terrifying man with a horrifying gaze that freezes those who lock eyes with him as the air around them turns ice cold. He wears a long, dark coat, and a top hat. It is said that he glides past graves and tombs as if his feet don't touch the ground.

LONDON, ENGLAND

EUROPE

The ghost of a crazed old woman haunts the cemetery looking for the children she murdered.

Many who have braved a stroll through the cemetery have seen glowing eyes.

This cemetery was once a place where mysterious men in dark robes held secret, spooky rituals.

Eltz Castle, Munstermaifeld, Germany

THE
HAUNTED
KNIGHT ARMOR

The past may still be alive in Eltz Castle. Hundreds of years ago, noble knights fought ferociously to protect everything within its stone walls. If you stumble down the wrong hall, you might hear the creepy clinks and clanks of ancient armor from the spirits that still yearn to defeat their enemies. Be careful not to get in their way, or you too may haunt the halls forever!

EUROPE

MUNSTERMAIFELD, GERMANY

One bedroom still displays the breastplate and battle-ax of a countess who died defending the castle. Many claim to have seen her ghost roaming the halls.

Built in 1157, hundreds of years later, the original family still owns the castle.

CRAZY CREEPY

Underwater Hauntings

Dive deep into the darkness to discover a haunted water world full of freaky phenomenon!

Shipwreck, SS Andrea Doria, Nantucket, Massachusetts, USA

This eerie underwater shipwreck is so deep in the ocean that people have died trying to reach it and explore it. Scuba divers have claimed to see apparitions in their peripheral vision and some have had the chilling sensation of being touched on their arms and legs. Many people believe there are souls still down there begging to be rescued.

NORTH AMERICA

NANTUCKET, MASSACHUSETTS, USA

Shipwreck, RMS Rhone, Salt Island, British Virgin Islands

This ship battled against a horrendous hurricane until it ultimately crashed and broke into two pieces! Scuba divers who have explored this shipwreck have reported seeing people frantically swimming up to the surface without scuba gear (which is very dangerous). When divers have approached these people to assist them, the frantic swimmers suddenly disappear without a trace.

CARIBBEAN ISLANDS

SALT ISLAND, BRITISH VIRGIN ISLANDS

CRAZY CREEPY

Underwater Hauntings

NORTH AMERICA

GINNIE SPRINGS, FL, USA

The Devil's Eye Cave, Ginnie Springs, Florida, USA

Don't be fooled by the beautiful colors within this one-of-a-kind scuba dive, or you might just get sucked in. It is believed that a vortex-like force exists inside this cave that makes divers disoriented and confused. Some say it is the spirit of a dead diver looking for help.

Underwater pumpkin carving contests during the month of October are becoming a tradition for many scuba divers in Florida!

"The Giant" Plane Wreck, Sardinia, Italy

The pilot and crew went down with this plane when it crashed, sinking to the bottom of the ocean. Scuba divers have reported seeing a pilot and crew in the cockpit. But it is said, as divers get closer, the pilot and crew suddenly vanish.

EUROPE

SARDINIA, ITALY

Kymlinge, Stockholm, Sweden

THE ZOMBIE TRAIN

Beware! If you accidently step on board the Silver Arrow train, you may be trapped on it—FOREVER. You just travel, and travel, and travel, for what seems like forever. Some say the Silver Arrow stops once a year at a half-built, abandoned train stop called Kymlinge, where only the dead get on and off. Any passengers on the train have expressionless, vacant looks, like motionless zombies.

EUROPE

STOCKHOLM, SWEDEN

Legend says the Silver Arrow can only be seen after midnight, traveling at a very high speed.

The Silver Arrow is also called "Silverpilen" in German.

31

Akershus Castle, Oslo, Norway

THE EVIL
GUARD DOG AND THE
PHANTOM HORSE

When taking a spooky stroll around this creepy castle, be sure to stay clear of the Maiden's Tower! This was the old main entrance of the castle, and it is said a big, black dog was buried there in the hopes that it would become a ghost that would guard the area. The dog was named Malcanisen, which means "the vicious dog" or "the evil dog." Legend also says that there is a horse that can be heard galloping around the old entrance, and if you see it, you will die by the end of the year.

EUROPE

OSLO, NORWAY

The ghost of a woman is often seen walking toward her chamber. She appears from the darkness wearing a long robe and has no facial features.

This castle was a prison where many executions were held and was constructed in a way that made it nearly impossible for enemies to invade.

Babenhausen Barracks,
Hesse, Germany

The GHOST
That Talks Backwards

Originally housing for German soldiers during WWII, this heart-thumping property is now a museum. In the middle of the night, you might hear the angry shouting of German commands, see the ghastly ghost of a German soldier, or hear footsteps right behind you. But to put the scary cherry on top of the paranormal pie, multiple people who have entered the museum have picked up a phone only to hear the spine-tingling voice of a woman talking backward.

EUROPE

HESSE, GERMANY

Legend says a witch was burned at the stake in town and her ghost is said to have killed several German soldiers.

Lights are known to turn on and off by themselves and voices can be heard in the basement.

Edinburgh Castle,
Edinburgh, Scotland

THE HEADLESS DRUMMER

Seeing this castle even from afar will give you goosebumps. Dozens of people sick with the Black Death were trapped below the castle to make sure the sickness didn't spread. Many of them died, their tortured souls still lurking in the shadows. If you can brave beyond the sea of spirits, you might encounter one of the most notorious ghosts of all: a lonely, headless drummer boy who seems to appear only when the castle is under attack. Don't let him think you are a threat, as there is no telling what he is capable of.

EUROPE

EDINBURGH,
SCOTLAND

A dog has been seen roaming the dog cemetery.

A piper wandered into the castle years ago and is said to have never returned. Listen carefully and you might hear his mysterious music.

CRAZY CREEPY

Straight-Up Scary

Take a break from the ghouls and ghosts—you don't need ghost vision to tell how terrifying these places are!

Creepy Crawly Caves (a.k.a. Gomantong Caves), Sabah, Malaysia

This cave is home to millions of bats, but that's not even the scary part. Cockroaches stampede the walls of the cave, blanketing nearly every inch, feeding off the hundreds of piles of bat poo (a.k.a. guano). Each pile is nearly a foot tall and accompanied by a terrifying number of parasites to boot. DO NOT GO IN THERE!

ASIA

SABAH, MALAYSIA

Snake Island, Ilha da Queimada Grande, Brazil

With 4,000 golden lancehead snakes, this island seems like a nightmare straight out of a storybook. The golden lancehead is the most venomous viper snake in the world—its venom is capable of melting human flesh! It is known as one of the world's deadliest islands and is banned to travelers. Not a good place to be whether you have ophidiophobia (fear of snakes) or not!

AFRICA

CAPE TOWN, SOUTH AFRICA

SOUTH AMERICA

ILHA DA QUEIMADA GRANDE, BRAZIL

Shark Alley, Gansbaai, South Africa

Between two islands off the coast of South Africa, you'll find the fearsome Shark Alley, a thin strip of water that is one of the most populated areas of great white sharks. They scope the alley in large numbers hoping to find their next bloody meal.

Xochimilco, Mexico

ISLAND
OF THE DOLLS,

Legend says the ghost of a girl who mysteriously drowned haunts this island, which is now covered in hundreds of terrifying dolls hanging from trees. The dolls were hung by a man who had moved to the island and wanted to soothe the ghost's unsettled spirit. He believed the first doll he hung belonged to the drowned girl and soon realized the doll was possessed by her. As he hung more dolls to please the ghost, those dolls became possessed by other dead children.

NORTH AMERICA

XOCHIMILCO, MEXICO

Tourists claim to have seen dolls' heads, arms, and eyes move.

The dolls are known to whisper as you walk by.

Westminster Presbyterian Churchyard, Baltimore, Maryland, USA

THE SCREAMING SKULL

This eerie cemetery is freaky at its finest. The story goes that a minister was murdered, but even after he died, his disembodied head never stopped screaming. The murderers gagged the skull and buried it in a block of cement in an attempt to quiet the screaming. But if you take a walk through the cemetery and listen very closely, the screaming skull can still be heard.

NORTH AMERICA

BALTIMORE, MARYLAND. USA

GENEVIEVE
WIFE OF
SAMUEL D. SHIPLEY
Died Jan. 10, 1892

MARY K
DIED MAY
AGED 76

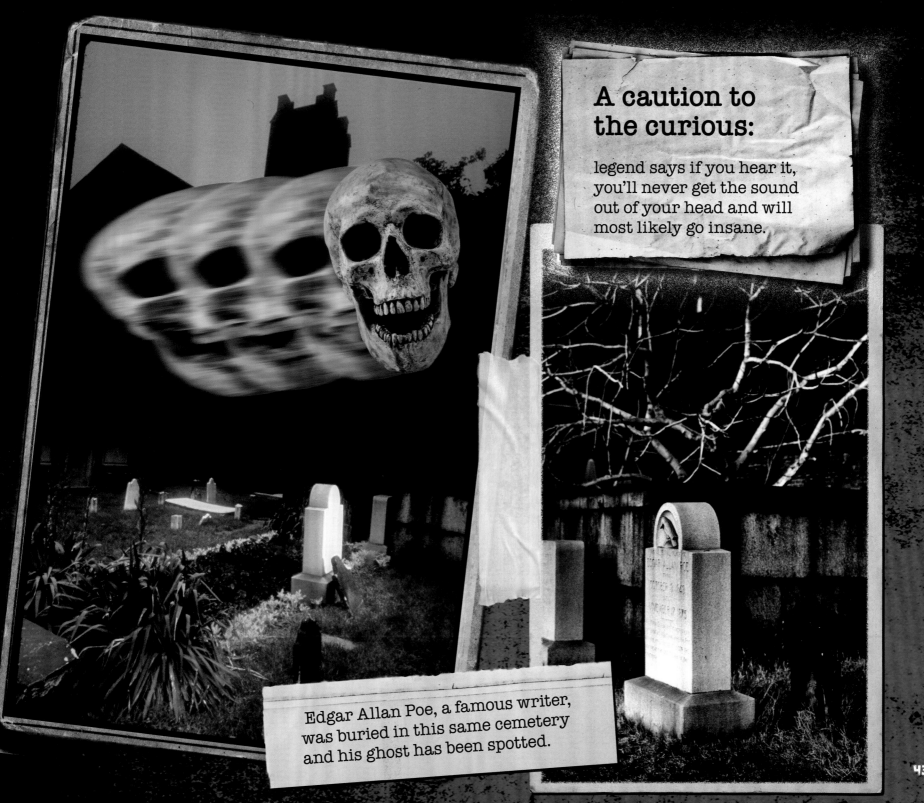

legend says if you hear it, you'll never get the sound out of your head and will most likely go insane.

Edgar Allan Poe, a famous writer, was buried in this same cemetery and his ghost has been spotted.

Skinwalker Ranch, Utah, USA

SHAPE-SHIFTER
TRICKSTER

A dangerous, shape-shifting creature known by local Native Americans as a skinwalker is said to terrorize this plot of land. Known as Skinwalker Ranch, many people stay clear of this land, but those who have been brave enough to live on the ranch have witnessed petrifying paranormal activity, including UFO sightings, crop circles, glowing orbs, and poltergeists.

NORTH AMERICA

UTAH, USA

Many cows on the ranch have mysteriously died or disappeared.

There is a movie based on this ranch.

A poltergeist is a ghost or spirit that shows its presence by making noises, knocking things over, and so on.

Stanley Hotel, Estes Park,
Colorado, USA

THE HAUNTED HOTEL

The haunted Stanley Hotel in
Colorado, USA, is hailed by paranormal
experts as one of the most active ghost
sites in the USA. At night, a chilling song
on the piano can be heard in the music
room, most likely played by the ghost
of Mrs. Stanley. Guests have reported
their bags mysteriously being unpacked,
lights turning off and on, and children's
laughter echoing through the halls.

NORTH
AMERICA

ESTES PARK,
COLORADO, USA

The ghost of Mr. Stanley is known to show up in pictures.

Steven King based his book *The Shining* on the hauntings in this hotel.

CRAZY CREEPY

Haunted USA National Parks

Over the years, rangers, tourists, and Native Americans have gathered many scary stories that take place in the USA's most beautiful places—National Parks!

NORTH AMERICA

NEW JERSEY, USA

NORTH AMERICA

PENNSYLVANIA, USA

Devil's Den, Gettysburg National Battlefield, Pennsylvania, USA

Inside this cob-webbed cave known as Devil's Den, countless visitors to the park have reported seeing a barefooted ghost known as the "Tennessean" or "the hippie." He carries a rifle and speaks to visitors, frequently pointing and saying, "What you're looking for is over there."

The Kangaroo Bat, New Jersey Pinelands National Park, New Jersey, USA

On the Batona Trail, visitors have described sightings of a freaky, kangaroo-like creature with the head of a dog, bat-like wings, horns, and a forked tail. The animal is said to prowl through the marshes and spook people with its hideous appearance. Residents of cities near the Pinelands have reported hearing the creepy creature's screams late at night.

The Witch of Great Smokey Mountains National Park, North Carolina, USA

On the Norton Creek Trail in the Great Smokey Mountains, there is a legend of a witch with a long, sharp finger made of stone. She is called Spearfinger and walks the trails disguised as an elderly woman who lures in children who have wandered too far from home.

NORTH AMERICA

NORTH CAROLINA, USA

CRAZY CREEPY

Haunted USA National Parks

NORTH AMERICA

CALIFORNIA, USA

NORTH AMERICA

ARIZONA, USA

The Boy Who Cries for Help, Yosemite National Park, California, USA

Hikers who visit Yosemite's Grouse Lake often report hearing a distinct wailing cry like the sound of a puppy. According to Native American folklore, the sound is the cry of a boy who drowned in the lake. Legend has it that he calls to hikers for help, but that anyone who ventures into the lake will be pulled under and drowned.

The Wailing Woman, Grand Canyon, Arizona, USA

Guests and park rangers have reported hearing a woman wailing in the night, only to find no one around. Some have even witnessed a glowing figure disappearing down canyon paths at night. Supposedly, it is the ghost of a woman who drowned her two children after the father of her children married another woman there.

SOUTH DAKOTA, USA

The Banshee and Her Pet, Badlands National Park, South Dakota, USA

By moonlight, the ghost of the banshee of the desert might be seen on a hill, her hair blowing and her arms tossing about wildly in different directions. Sometimes she has a pet skeleton with her that haunts the area in search of music. If he hears music, he will sit outside the door and nod with the beat. If there is a violin within his reach, he will play it through half the night.

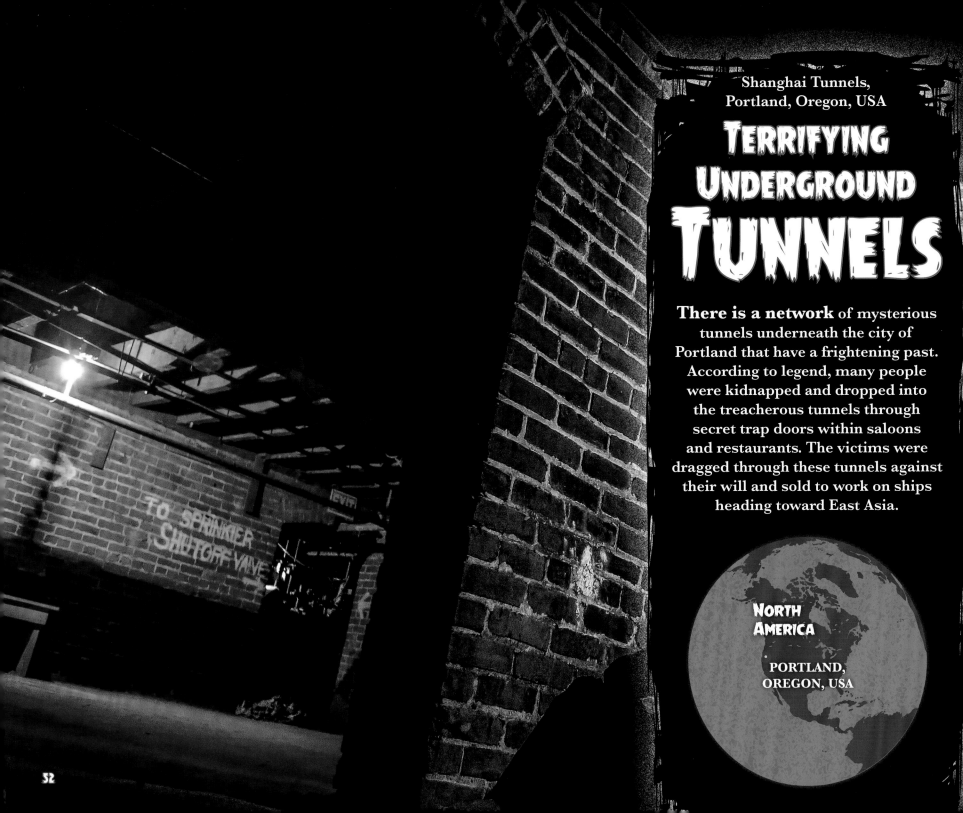

Shanghai Tunnels,
Portland, Oregon, USA

TERRIFYING UNDERGROUND TUNNELS

There is a network of mysterious tunnels underneath the city of Portland that have a frightening past. According to legend, many people were kidnapped and dropped into the treacherous tunnels through secret trap doors within saloons and restaurants. The victims were dragged through these tunnels against their will and sold to work on ships heading toward East Asia.

NORTH AMERICA

PORTLAND, OREGON, USA

Some men worked for several years before finding a way to get back home.

Some fought back and died. Others died after being held captive for so long. Their ghosts linger in the depths of the tunnels.

Whaley House, San Diego,
California, USA

The Most
Haunted
House of All

The Whaley House is known as
the number-one most haunted house
in the USA. People have reported
seeing the ghost of Thomas Whaley
on the upper roof of the house, Anna
Whaley in the downstairs room or in
the garden, and the ghost of a girl in
the dining room.

**NORTH
AMERICA**

**SAN DIEGO,
CALIFORNIA, USA**

WANTED

YANKEE JIM
DEAD OR ALIVE

A small dog has been seen running down the halls with its ears flapping.

Before the Whaleys owned the house, a man was hung on the property. His ghost is known as "Yankee Jim." It is said his boots can be heard dragging through the house.

Manchac Swamp, Frenier,
Louisiana, USA

THE CURSE OF THE VOODOO QUEEN

Take a wild walk around this scary swamp and you may find the spirit of a voodoo queen freakishly floating across the steamy water or strumming her guitar and eerily singing by the edge. But it's not just her tortured soul that lingers there. Dozens of other souls she cursed when she felt taken for granted after helping many of the townsfolk dwell in the murky depths.

NORTH AMERICA

**FRENIER,
LOUISIANA, USA**

Legend says her curse came true when a horrendous hurricane swept through the area on the day of her funeral and killed everyone around.

Chauchilla Cemetery, Nazca, Peru

THE HAIRY MUMMY GRAVE ROBBERS

These mysterious mummies are not wearing wigs—they wear the hair of their original bodies from 1,200 years ago, leaving their bodies strangely and suspiciously lifelike for those that pass by. When the ancient burial site was discovered in the 1920s, it was clear that grave robbers had sifted through the skeletons and stolen many of the artifacts. Many of the artifacts have since been returned, but will the hairy mummies ever get their revenge on those rascally robbers?

SOUTH AMERICA

NAZCA, PERU

This is the only site in Peru in which ancient mummies are seen in their original graves.

CRAZY CREEPY

Freaky Festivals

Check out these spooky celebrations inspired by the dead and dreadful!

Hungry Ghost Festival, China

The Hungry Ghost Festival is celebrated on the 15th day of the seventh month on the Lunar Calendar, July or August on the western calendar. It is a time when the spirits of those who were not given a proper tribute at death may return. Families burn incense and gold paper to soothe the spirits. Tables of food are set out for wandering ghosts, and live shows are held with the first row of seats reserved for the dead. On the final day of the festival, paper boats are lit and put in water to guide the ghosts back to the underworld. When the flames go out, the spirit attached to the boat crosses over back into the afterlife.

ASIA

CHINA

Mothman Festival, Point Pleasant, West Virginia, USA

Every year, Point Pleasant celebrates a strange creature called Mothman. Suspiciously similar to the creature that appeared in Pripyat years later (see p. 17), Mothman is also a large, bird-like creature with a 15-foot (4.57-m) wing span and glowing red eyes. People reported sights of Mothman in the year leading up to a bridge collapsing in the town. During the festival, people dress up as Mothman, ride hayrides at the Mothman Museum, take pictures with the Mothman statue, and participate in other spooky events.

NORTH AMERICA

POINT PLEASANT, WEST VIRGINIA, USA

NORTH
AMERICA

MANITOU SPRINGS,
COLORADO, USA

Emma Crawford Coffin Races, Manitou Springs, Colorado, USA

Each year, Manitou Springs hosts at least seventy teams in a coffin race competition. Each team consists of a person who sits in a coffin, and four people, two on either side of the coffin, who race the coffin down Manitou Avenue. The coffin races were inspired by the local legend of Emma Crawford, who lived in the town of Manitou Springs 100 years ago. She was buried on top a mountain that loomed over the tiny town. Years later, a wild rain storm washed Emma's coffin down the side of the mountain.

CRAZY CREEPY
Freaky Festivals

Day of the Dead, Mexico

In this bone-tingling festival, skeletons big and small roam the streets, and brightly colored items, skeletons, and masks are worn. Altars are decorated with flowers, food, toys, sweets, and utensils to honor the spirits of the dead. Delectably sweet and spooky sugar skulls are given as gifts.

NORTH AMERICA

MEXICO

Photo Credits: